THE ANTI-INFLAMMATORY VITAMIN MADE EASY

A Beginner's Guide On How To Stop Chronic
Inflammation With Vitamin D Supplements

Happy Health Publishing

THANK YOU FOR YOUR PURCHASE!

DO YOU LIKE HAPPY HEALTH PUBLISHING?
SUBSCRIBE TO OUR NEWSLETTER AND
DOWNLOAD YOUR FREE GIFT NOW!

IT WILL HELP YOU LIVE YOUR BEST LIFE AND
CLAIM YOUR PERSONAL POWERS!

https:// l.ead.me/hhp-free-gift

TABLE OF CONTENTS

INTRODUCTION

The body's normal reaction to protect itself from damage is defined as inflammation and it is involved in the process of wound healing. It is a broad concept that originally referred to a series of 5 definitive symptoms and signs such as being red, heat, swelling, aching, and functional disturbance.[1] Inflammation is divided into two types: acute and chronic. Acute inflammation typically lasts for a short period of time. It usually resolves in 14 days or less and symptoms arise rapidly. This form returns the body to its pre-injury or disease state. Chronic inflammation is a slow and less serious type of inflammation. It normally lasts for more than 1 month. It can happen even when there is no damage, and it does not necessarily resolve when the irritant or wound is healed. Chronic inflammation has been associated with autoimmune diseases, as well as long-term stress.

VITAMIN D

Vitamin D is considered one of the fat-soluble vitamins that helps with the metabolism of bone and appears to have anti-inflammatory and immune-modulating functions.[2] Vitamin D was first described as a vitamin in the twentieth century, is now known as a prohormone. Vitamin D is classified into two forms: vitamin D2 and D3. Ultraviolet exposure of provitamin D2 in fungi yeast produces vitamin D2, while ultraviolet exposure of provitamin D3 in the skin produces vitamin D3.[3] Despite the fact that food is fortified with vitamin D, rickets still persists, a deficiency of which remains a major problem for health professionals. Vitamin D deficiency in childhood can lead to rickets, as well as a high risk of bone malformations and bone fractures. The primary form of vitamin D is 25-hydroxyvitamin D. However, the biologically active form of vitamin D was found to be 1,25-dihydroxyvitamin D. In fact, studies have shown that vitamin D3 is more active than vitamin D2. The most interesting role of vitamin D is to reduce the risk of developing chronic diseases, including cancer, autoimmune, infectious, and cardiovascular diseases. Moreover, recent studies have found associations between vitamin D deficiency and inflammation.[4] Vitamin D deficiency increases the risk of type 1 diabetes and Crohn's disease. An increased need for vitamin D in pregnant women is thought to reduce the production of antibodies against fetal pancreatic islet cells. Studies have shown that vitamin D deficiency increases insulin resistance and reduces insulin production, which in turn leads to metabolic syndrome. Another study has shown that a combination of 1200 mg of calcium and vitamin D 800IU reduces type 2 diabetes by 33%.

Vitamin D's primary function is to sustain and control the body's level of calcium, it is essential for the development of a healthy bone. As a result, vitamin D deficiency not only increases the tendency of developing the bone disease, but it has been related to a higher risk of developing elevated blood pressure, cancer, autoimmune disorders, inflammatory disorders, and type 2 diabetes.[6] As mentioned above, Ultraviolet sunlight allows vitamin D to be synthesized in the skin. However, the requisite ultraviolet waves are only released in areas below 35° latitude all year. As a result, vitamin

D intake is critical, however, vitamin D is normally found in a few food sources including oily fish (30 µg per 100g), eggs (1.75 µg per 100g), and meat (0.6 µg per 100g). For healthy people, a range of 20-50 ng/mL is considered sufficient. Vitamin D inadequacy is indicated by a level of below 12 ng/mL. Also, vitamin D inadequacy affects nearly half of the world's population and it affects an estimated 1 billion people worldwide, including all age groups and ethnicities.[7] Vitamin D insufficiency is caused by lifestyle and environmental factors (such as reduced outdoor activities, air pollution) that reduce sunlight exposure, which is necessary for UVB-induced vitamin D synthesis in the human skin. There is a high risk of vitamin D deficiency depending on a country's geographical location due to a lack of access to vitamin D from the sun's ultraviolet rays and a relatively poor level of vitamin D in food. Vitamin D deficiency can be caused by a number of factors, including reduced skin synthesis, decreased vitamin D absorption, kidney disease, and hereditary disorders. Also, there are groups at risk of vitamin D deficiency including breastfed infants, pregnant women, and older people. Thus, these people should take vitamin D supplements to maintain normal blood levels. Vitamin D toxicity is extremely rare but can occur accidentally with foods high in vitamin D or vitamin D supplements. When vitamin D is administered daily at a dose of 50,000 IU or more, levels of vitamin D above 150 ng/ml (374 nmol/l) can lead to vitamin D toxicity, hypercalcemia, and hyperphosphatemia. Also, an overdose of vitamin D can lead to acute poisoning, loss of appetite, vomiting, diarrhea, malaise, and impaired renal function.

DEFINITION AND PREVALENCE OF VITAMIN D DEFICIENCY

Although the exact amount of 25-hydroxyvitamin D in serum has not been determined, most experts have identified vitamin D deficiency as a serum level of less than 20 ng/ml (50 nmol/l). Also, some experts believe that less than 32 ng/ml of serum levels of 25-hydroxyvitamin D can lead to loss of intestinal absorption, and less than that can lead to vitamin D deficiency. If it is not possible to determine the amount of 25-hydroxyvitamin D, it can be considered a vitamin D deficiency if the parathyroid hormone (PTH) level is more than 30-40 ng/ml (75-100 nmol/l). This is because vitamin D deficiency significantly reduces the amount of calcium and phosphorus absorbed from the small intestine into the bloodstream, which in turn lowers the levels of calcium and phosphorus in the blood, increasing thyroid hormone production in the thyroid gland and releasing calcium and phosphate from the bones. Thus, when bone calcium and phosphorus are reduced, the bones become thinner and become softer. In women, an average increase in 25-hydroxyvitamin D levels from 20 to 32 ng/ml (50 to 80 nmol/l) increases intestinal calcium absorption by 45% to

65%. Vitamin D toxicity is thought to occur if the serum level of 25-hydroxyvitamin D is 150 ng/ml (374 nmol/l) or higher. According to epidemiological studies, serum levels of 25-hydroxyvitamin D are less than 20 ng/ml, and there are more than 1 billion people in the world with vitamin D deficiency. Studies show that vitamin D deficiency is 40-100% among older men and women in the United States and Europe. Fifty percent of postmenopausal women have osteoporosis, with serum levels of 25-hydroxyvitamin D are below 30 ng/ml (75 nmol/l). People living around the equator are exposed to a lot of sunlight, so a 25-hydroxyvitamin D level above 30 ng/ml is considered a normal level. On the other hand, in Saudi Arabia, the United Arab Emirates, Australia, Turkey, India, and Lebanon, 30-50% of children and adults have levels of 25-hydroxyvitamin D below 20 ng/ml. In addition, pregnant and breastfeeding mothers are at high risk for vitamin D deficiency, so they should take a multivitamin containing 400 IU daily. Postpartum vitamin D deficiency occurs in 80% of infants and 73% of mothers.

THE NORMAL RANGE OF VITAMIN D IN BLOOD

Vitamin D status	Blood levels (ng/mL)	Blood levels (nmol/L)
Severe deficiency	<10	<25
Deficiency	10-20	25-50
Insufficiency	20-30	50-75
Normal	>30	>75
Excess	>100	>250

According to the study, the daily recommended dose of Vitamin D is 200 IU for children and adults under 50, 400 IU for 51-70 years, and 600 IU for 71 years and older. Experts believe that the daily dose for children and adults who are not exposed to the sun should be 800IU-1000IU. Breast milk contains very small amounts of vitamin D (approximately 20IU/l), and if the mother is deficient in vitamin D, the infant will receive less vitamin D. When a mother is given 4,000 IU/day of vitamin D3, the amount of 25-hydroxyvitamin D increases by more than 30 ng ml, which is enough for infant to take adequate amount of vitamin D. In Canada, guidelines have been developed to prevent vitamin D deficiency in infants and children with a daily dose of 400 IU of vitamin D3. The study followed 78,000 people in Austria for 20 years and found that adults with low levels of vitamin D in their blood were three times more likely to die than those with normal levels. In more detail, the cause of death was related to the amount of vitamin D and complications of diabetes mellitus. Preliminary results of this study were presented at a meeting of the European Diabetes Research Association on September 20, 2019, and experts point out that it is too early to conclude that vitamin D deficiency shortens people's life expectancy. However, vitamin D deficiency has been shown to adversely affect bone strength. It has also been shown to increase the risk of autoimmune diseases such as diabetes, high blood pressure, some cancers, and diffuse cirrhosis. The stereotype that vitamin D plays an important role in bone health and calcium absorption has changed rapidly in recent years and has become more widespread. However, it remains unclear whether dietary supplements and vitamin D supplements are necessary to prevent some chronic diseases and to live a healthy and long life. A recent article in the New England Journal of Medicine found that vitamin D supplements were ineffective in preventing type 2 diabetes in high-risk groups. However, some researchers have suggested that vitamin

D supplementation at an older age may not be sufficient to prevent disease. This is because the foundations of many diseases, such as diabetes, are laid at a young age. This is because many diseases, such as diabetes mellitus, begin at a young age. The research team found a link between vitamin D levels and the risk of dying before the age of 60. People with a blood vitamin D level of less than 10 nmol/L had a nearly three-fold higher risk of death during the study than those with a level of 50 nmol/L. Although the cause remains unclear, studies have shown that the level of vitamin D in the blood is related to diabetes mellitus. Vitamin D has a hormone-like effect on the body and is involved in regulating the immune system. Type 1 diabetes is an autoimmune disorder and is thought to be related to vitamin D levels. Vitamin D also plays an important role in the function of cells that secrete insulin, which regulates blood sugar levels. It is associated with type 2 diabetes because it determines the body's sensitivity to insulin. Therefore, children and young people need to prevent vitamin D deficiency and get the right amount of vitamin D. The guidelines of the International Endocrine Society recommend that adults should take 1,500 to 2,000 IU per day, and children and adolescents should

take 600 to 1,000 IU per day.

VITAMIN D DEFICIENCY AND CHRONIC DISEASES

CANCER

Epidemiological studies have shown that serum levels of 25-hydroxyvitamin D below 20 ng/ml increase the risk of several cancers such as colorectal, prostate, and breast cancer by 30-50%. Specific genes control the expression of the 25-hydroxyvitamin D-1α-hydroxylase enzyme and the 1,25-dihydroxyvitamin D receptor in the colon, prostate, breast, and other tissues to maintain normal cell regeneration and differentiation and prevent cancer. 1,25-dihydroxyvitamin D stimulates apoptosis and controls angiogenesis because limiting the energy of the cancer cell can lead to a lack of energy in the cancer cell and its ability to survive. It remains unclear that the regulation of 1,25-dihydroxyvitamin D in the kidneys and why vitamin D, which is produced by sunlight, stops at a certain level.

CARDIOVASCULAR DISEASE

There is a high risk of high blood pressure and cardiovascular disease in areas with vitamin D deficiency. Studies have shown that when a patient with high blood pressure is exposed to sunlight for 3 hours a week for 3 months, the amount of 25-hydroxyvitamin D increases by 180%, systolic and diastolic blood pressure decreases by 6 mmHg, and blood pressure stabilizes. Vitamin D deficiency exacerbates heart failure and increases the risk of atherosclerosis by increasing the levels of C-reactive protein and interleukin-10 in the blood.

CHRONIC KIDNEY DISEASE (CKD)

The guidelines for the treatment of kidney disease recommend that serum levels of 25-hydroxyvitamin D should be more than 30 ng/mL, in any stage of chronic kidney disease. Vitamin D and its active analogs should never be given to a patient, regardless of the level of parathyroid hormone and the stage of renal insufficiency. This is because patients with late-stage chronic kidney disease reduce 1,25-dihydroxyvitamin D when the glomerular filtration rate is less than <30ml/min/1.73m2, and a decrease in vitamin D production leads to hypocalcemia and increases parathyroid hormone levels. All this increases the risk of kidney and bone diseases.

AUTOIMMUNE DISEASES, OSTEOARTHRITIS, AND DIABETES

Vitamin D deficiency increases the risk of type 1 diabetes and Crohn's disease. In clinical observation, patients with rheumatoid arthritis and osteoarthritis were deficient in this vitamin. Various studies have shown that children taking vitamin D supplements have a lower risk of developing type 1 diabetes.

CALCIUM, PHOSPHORUS, AND BONE METABOLISM

The digestive system can absorb only 10-15% of the calcium and 60% of the phosphorus in the diet without the effects of vitamin D. One of the main functions of vitamin D is to promote the absorption of calcium and phosphorus through the small intestine into the bloodstream. 1.25-dihydroxyvitamin D interacts with its own vitamin D receptor to increase calcium absorption in the small intestine by 30-40% and phosphorus absorption by approximately 80%. Serum levels of 30 ng/ml or less of 25-hydroxyvitamin D increase the levels of parathyroid hormone and decrease intestinal calcium absorption. Parathyroid hormone increases the production of 1,25-hydroxyvitamin D and the reabsorption of calcium in the kidneys. As mentioned above, due to vitamin D deficiency, the parathyroid gland senses the amount of calcium and phosphorus in the blood and releases calcium and phosphorus from the bones into the bloodstream to compensate for the amount of calcium and phosphorus in the blood. The parathyroid hormone activates osteoblast cells and converts them from osteoclast precursors to mature osteoclast cells. Mature osteoclasts dissolve mineralized collagen in bone tissue and release calcium and phosphorus into the blood. As a result, the bones become softer, thinner. Vitamin D deficiency is harmful, but it has the advantage of preventing excessive calcium mineralization and calcification in the skeleton. When vitamin D deficiency worsens, the parathyroid gland becomes overactive, causing secondary hyperparathyroidism. Conversely, when hypomagnesemia occurs, thyroid hormone levels return to normal, and levels of 25-hydroxyvitamin D reduce to less than 20 ng/ml. Parathyroid hormone has the advantage of converting 25-hydroxyvitamin D to 1,25-dihydroxyvitamin D, but increasing metabolism reduces the amount of 25-hydroxyvitamin D in the serum and exacerbates vitamin D deficiency. The parathyroid hormones also reduce phosphorus levels by phosphaturia. Thus, a decrease in the amount and production of calcium-phosphorus reduces the mineralization of tissue collagen, which is a major factor in the development of rickets in children and osteoporosis in adults.

OSTEOPOROSIS AND FRACTURES

Vitamin D deficiency can lead to osteoporosis. According to the study, 33% of women aged 60-70 and 66% of men aged 80 and over have osteoporosis. In addition, 47% of women and 22% of men aged 50 and over have fractures due to osteoporosis. According to the study, women were given 1,200 mg of calcium and 800 IU of vitamin D3 daily for 3 years, resulted reducing bone fractures by 43%. Studies show that the daily consumption of 700-800 IU of vitamin D3 reduces bone marrow fractures by 26%.

MUSCLE STRENGTH AND WEAKNESS

Vitamin D deficiency can lead to muscle weakness. Skeletal muscle has a vitamin D receptor, and vitamin D is essential after a large amount of physical activity. Increasing serum levels of 25-

hydroxyvitamin D above 40 ng/ml significantly improves muscle strength. Vitamin D3 of 400IU per day did not improve muscle weakness, but increasing the dose of vitamin D3 in combination with calcium at a dose of 800IU per day improved muscle weakness. Studies have shown that taking 800IU of vitamin D2 and calcium supplements for five months reduces muscle weakness by 72%.

RECOMMENDATION FOR VITAMIN D INTAKE

According to the Institute of Medicine, the daily dose of Vitamin D is 400IU for children under 12 months, and 600IU for adults under 70, 800IU for 70 years and older.

Age or condition	Institute of Medicine	
	Adequate intake (IU/day)	Upper limit (IU/day)
0-12 months	400	1000-1500
1-18 years	600	2500-4000
years	600	4000
>70 years	800	4000
Pregnancy	600	4000
Lactation	600	4000

INFLAMMATION

SYMPTOMS OF INFLAMMATION

Acute and chronic diseases, certain drugs, and various external stimuli can cause inflammation. The main inflammation signs are being red, heat, swelling, aching, and functional disturbance. Long-term inflammation may cause a range of symptoms and have a wide-ranging effect on the body. Chronic inflammation can cause the following symptoms: body ache, exhaustion, insomnia, anxiety, depression, other mood disorders, gastrointestinal symptoms including constipation, diarrhea, acid reflux, weight gain, and recurrent infections. Also, the symptoms vary depending on the location of the site of inflammation. In rheumatoid arthritis, joints are attacked by the immune system, thus patients may experience loss of joint function, fatigue, limited range of motion, and fatigue. On the other hand, in inflammatory bowel disease, the digestive system is affected by inflammation, thus it causes weight loss, stomach pain, diarrhea, and anemia.

HOW TO OBTAIN BLOOD TESTS TO CHECK LEVELS OF INFLAMMATION

There is no one test for diagnosing inflammation of the factors that cause it. However, there are few markers that may assist in the diagnosis of inflammation. Serum protein electrophoresis is thought to be the most effective method of confirming chronic inflammation. It detects problems by measuring specific proteins in the liquid portion of the blood. Excess or deficiency of these proteins may indicate inflammation as well as markers for other diseases. C-reactive protein, or CRP, is a highly sensitive protein in the blood that responds more quickly to tissue damage. The presence of reactive proteins in the blood plasma is a sign of inflammatory processes, damage, and the entry of foreign microorganisms such as bacteria, parasites, and fungi into the body. C-reactive protein stimulates the body's immune response and activates the immune system. Plasma levels of 0.5 mg/L of C-reactive protein are considered normal. In humans, the inflammatory process begins 4 to 6 hours after infection, and C-reactive protein levels begin to rise. The more acute the inflammatory process and the more active the disease, the higher the level of CRP in the blood. However, when the chronic form of the disease subsides, the level of CRP in the blood decreases sharply and increases again when it flares up. C-reactive protein results are used in the diagnosis of acute infectious diseases and also used to monitor the medical treatment process and the effectiveness of antibacterial therapy. The hsCRP (high-sensitivity CRP) test can detect the level of C-reactive protein and erythrocyte sedimentation rate which are inflammatory markers. Inflammation also increases erythrocyte sedimentation rate, but C-reactive protein is increased more rapidly. Researchers discovered that men with an elevated level of CRP (2mg/L) had thrice the tendency of developing heart disease and two times the risk of developing stroke compared to those with lower levels of C-reactive protein. Furthermore, the majority of inflammatory marker research is focused on cytokines including IL-1, 12, 18, and TNF-α.[8] Also, C-reactive protein is excreted by the liver into the bloodstream after tissue injury, infection, or inflammation. This test is not for diagnostic purposes but is ordered to control inflammation. Biochemical analysis of C-reactive protein may show an increase in the level of C-reactive protein in the blood in the following cases: rheumatic diseases, gastrointestinal disorders, heart attack, neonatal sepsis, tuberculosis, meningitis, and postoperative complications. Also, female sex hormones and contraceptive pills increase the levels of C-reactive protein. C reactive protein test is ordered for several conditions including bacterial infections, fungal infections, pelvic inflammatory disease, chronic inflammation, abdominal inflammation, and autoimmune diseases. Although the C-reactive protein test is not specific enough to diagnose any disease, it can determine the presence of general inflammation and infection and the need for treatment.

Researchers have identified complex molecular occurrences that happen when inflammation is inhibited by vitamin D. In this study, vitamin D deficient patients with asthma bronchitis, carcinoma of the prostate, and rheumatoid arthritis, benefited from vitamin D supplementation to raise blood vitamin D levels above 30ng/mL.[9] Receptors associated with the active form of vitamin D are found in the brain, prostate, breast, colon, and immune cells, and are capable of producing the enzyme 25-hydroxyvitamin d-1α-hydroxylase. More than 200 genes, directly and indirectly, control the expression of receptors and enzymes in these tissues and regulate regeneration, differentiation, apoptosis, and angiogenesis. In clinical practice, [1.25 (OH)2D] is used to regulate the development and division of cells and its analogs are used in the treatment of psoriasis. One of the main functions of [1,25(OH)2D] is to enhance immunity through monocytes and macrophages. Monocytes and macrophages contain vitamin D receptors and 25-hydroxyvitamin D-1α-hydroxylase enzyme genes. When these cells are activated by a foreign antigen, the expression of these genes is intensified, resulting in the formation of 1,25 (OH) 2D, which in turn produces cathelicidin, which is capable of degrading and destroying TB and other bacteria. It is believed that this specific antimicrobial is synthesized only by the effect of [1.25(OH)2D]. If the serum level of [1.25 (OH)D] is less than 20 ng/ml (50 nmol/l) or vitamin D deficiency is impaired, the bactericidal activity of monocytes and macrophages is impaired and there is a high risk of mycobacterium tuberculosis and other chronic infections. Therefore, vitamin D is essential for the treatment of chronic infections and tuberculosis. 1,25 (OH) 2D also inhibits renal renin production, stabilizes arterial pressure, increases insulin production, lowers blood sugar to a stable level, and improves heart contraction and diastolic function.

MAGNESIUM

Magnesium is the human body's 4th abundant mineral and found in bone, soft tissues, blood, and muscles. According to studies, children with magnesium deficiency were shown to have elevated CRP, blood glucose, triglyceride, and insulin levels. Moreover, rich-magnesium foods including chocolate and oily fish, and taking magnesium supplements may help to reduce inflammation.[10] The symptoms of magnesium deficiency are nausea, vomiting, fatigue, loss of appetite, weakness, muscle twitch, and cramps. Low levels of magnesium in the blood are caused by gastrointestinal disorders, diabetes mellitus, low levels of thyroid hormones, long-term use of diuretics, and severe burns. Conversely, high levels of magnesium in the blood are caused by kidney failure, excessive secretion of parathyroid hormones, dehydration, diabetic acidosis, Addison's disease, and use of magnesium-containing laxatives and antacids. Because magnesium is an electrolyte, it is more effective to test it with other electrolytes such as sodium, potassium, chloride, bicarbonate, calcium, and phosphorus. When magnesium is low, potassium is often low and the magnesium levels are lowest during the first four to nine months of pregnancy.

VITAMIN A

Vitamin A is known as one of the fat-soluble vitamins that play a role in immune system regulation, eye vision, and maintenance of the reproduction system. Vitamin A is classified into two forms: preformed vitamin A which is found in animal sources and provitamin A carotenoids which are present in vegetables. According to studies, vitamin A prevents the overreaction of the immune system and inflammation.[11] The dietary recommendation for vitamin A intake is 700-900mcg/day for adults.[12] The symptoms of vitamin A deficiency are dry skin, dry eyes, night blindness, infertility and trouble conceiving, delayed growth, throat and chest infections, poor wound healing, and skin diseases. Vitamin A deficiency is a public health problem in many developing countries around the world. Globally, 3.3 million people have been diagnosed with vitamin A deficiency, and the majority of which occur in Southeast Asia.

VITAMIN K2

Vitamin K1 is found in plant-based foods, while vitamin K2 is found in foods from animal sources including liver, chicken, and eggs. The activity of proteins involved in blood clotting, metabolism of calcium, bone, and heart health is stimulated by vitamin K. Also, promoting the calcification of the skeleton and preventing the calcification of kidneys and blood vessels by regulating calcium deposition is one of the important functions of vitamin K. The dietary recommendations for vitamin K consumption in the United States are 90 μg/day for women and 120 μg/day for men.[12] According to research, inflammation of rheumatoid arthritis is reduced by supplementation of vitamin K2 which lowers levels of C-reactive protein.[13] The symptoms of vitamin

K2 deficiency are bleeding, losing bone strength, heart issues, easy bruising, heavy menstrual periods, and blood in urine or stool.

ANTI-INFLAMMATORY

ANTI-INFLAMMATORY DIET

Eating less toxic and more anti-inflammatory foods is crucial to reduce inflammation. Also, it is vital to avoid processed foods in favor of whole and antioxidant-based nutrient-dense foods. Antioxidants reduce free radical molecules which are the main triggers of inflammation. The Mediterranean diet is considered one of the anti-inflammatory diets which decrease inflammatory markers including C-reactive protein and interleukin-6.[14] Furthermore, low-carb and vegetarian diets are associated with a reduction in inflammation.[15, 16]

ANTI-INFLAMMATORY SUPPLEMENTS

1. ALPHA-LIPOIC ACID

Numerous studies showed that alpha-lipoic acid helps to reduce inflammatory marker levels, such as Interleukin 6 and Intercellular

Adhesion Molecule-1. The dietary recommendation for alpha-lipoic acid intake is 300 to 600mg/day for adults.[17]

2. CURCUMIN

It is a part of turmeric and also helps to improve arthritis and reduce the inflammation process.[18] The dietary recommendation for curcumin intake is 300 to 600mg/day.

3. FISH OIL

Omega-3 fatty acids are the main component of fish oil and reduce the inflammation process linked to chronic diseases. The dietary recommendation for Omega-3 fatty acid intake is 1.5g daily.

4. GINGER

According to one study, cancer patients who take ginger supplements had lower levels of CRP, and interleukin-6.[19] 1g daily is the recommended dosage for ginger.

5. RESVERATROL

It found in grapes and berries, also taking 500g daily showed improvement in markers of inflammation including Tumor necrosis factor and C-reactive protein.

6. SPIRULINA

Numerous studies showed that spirulina reduces inflammation and improves immunity.[20]

EXERCISES

Fat deposition in internal organs caused by lack of exercise activates several inflammatory processes. Physical inactivity promotes the development of several diseases including obesity, diabetes mellitus, and atherosclerosis. The beneficial effect of physical activity against inflammatory diseases can be attributed to the anti-inflammatory effects of daily physical activity. Regular exercise prevents several diseases including chronic inflammation, cancer, diabetes mellitus, cardiovascular diseases, chronic pulmonary obstructive disease, and depression. According to World Health Organization, adults should do a minimum of 150-300 minutes of exercise a week in order to maintain a healthy and active lifestyle.

Anti-inflammatory foods

ANTI-INFLAMMATORY FOODS

1. AVOCADOS

Avocados contain a variety of anti-inflammatory components

including tocopherols and carotenoids which can reduce

inflammation. According to one study, consuming avocado with a slice

of bread reduced inflammatory markers compared to people who

don't consume it.

2. BERRIES

There are several types of berries including blueberries, raspberries,

blackberries, and strawberries. Anthocyanins are a type of

antioxidants found in berries that are considered to have an anti-inflammatory effect. Natural killer cells are produced by the human body and have an important role in inflammation. In one study, people who ate berries on a daily basis had more natural killer cells and fewer anti-inflammatory markers than people who don't consume it every day.

3. BROCCOLI

Broccoli is high in nutrients and contains antioxidants such as sulforaphane which have an effect against inflammation. According to research, consuming more broccoli can reduce inflammation by decreasing Nuclear factor-kappa B and cytokine levels.

4. CHERRIES

Cherries are high in anti-inflammatory antioxidants including catechins and anthocyanins. In a research study, consuming approximately 300g cherries every day for 30 days, reduced inflammatory markers such as C-reactive protein and it remained stable for 30 days.

5. DARK CHOCOLATE AND COCOA

Cocoa and dark chocolates contain flavanols that have an anti-inflammatory effect and maintains the integrity of blood vessels by affecting endothelial cells. According to one study, eating dark chocolate improved the activity of endothelial cells significantly in smokers reduced inflammation.

6. FATTY FISH

Fatty fish are rich in eicosapentaenoic and docosahexaenoic acids which can reduce inflammatory markers. In one study, taking supplements of these acids, reduced C-reactive protein levels significantly.

7. GRAPES

Grapes contain anthocyanins and resveratrol which are considered anti-inflammatory compounds. According to research, consuming the extract of grape every day reduced chronic inflammation and the risk of diseases by decreasing Nuclear factor-kappa B.

8. GREEN TEA

Green tea contains epigallocatechin-3-gallate, one form of catechin which decreases inflammation by lowering several inflammatory cytokines.

9. EDIBLE MUSHROOMS

There are several types of edible mushrooms including shiitake, portobello, and truffles mushrooms which are high in nutrients and vitamins. Mushrooms contain antioxidants such as phenol which has an effect against inflammation. According to one study, they are best consumed partly fried or raw because cooking destroys the anti-inflammatory compounds.

10. EXTRA VIRGIN OLIVE OIL

Extra virgin olive oil contains monounsaturated fats, antioxidants and is the main component of the Mediterranean diet. According to a study related to the Mediterranean diet, consuming 50 ml olive oil every day reduced inflammatory markers and C-reactive protein levels.

11. PEPPERS

Peppers are rich in antioxidants and vitamins that have an effect against inflammation. Also, ferulic and sinapic acids found in chili peppers, decrease inflammation markers significantly.

12. TURMERIC

As mentioned above, it contains curcumin that is considered a strong anti-inflammatory compound. According to a study, in patients with metabolic syndrome, 1-gram curcumin with black pepper resulted in a substantial decrease in inflammation by reducing C-reactive protein levels.

13. TOMATOES

Tomatoes contain antioxidants and strong anti-inflammatory substances including potassium, vitamins, and lycopene. Lycopene can be helpful in lowering inflammatory markers linked to different forms of cancer.

INFLAMMATORY FOODS TO AVOID

In addition to eating a balanced diet, it is important to reduce the intake of inflammatory foods. Processed foods, such as junk foods, fried foods, refined carbohydrates, sweetened beverages, trans fats, and processed meats have been linked to increased C-reactive protein. The following foods have been related to the promotion of the inflammatory process.

1. Junk foods: pizza, hamburgers, salted snack foods, sweet desserts, candy, tacos, fried fast food, sugary beverages

2. Refined carbohydrates: pasta, white bread, white rice, snack foods

3. Fried foods: French fries, chicken, potato croquettes

4. Sugar-sweetened beverages: sports drinks, sweetened water, soda, fruit drinks

5. Processed meat: sausages. hotdogs, salami

6. Trans fats:pastries, desserts, pasta, onion rings

REFERENCES:

1.   Punchard NA, Whelan CJ, Adcock I. The Journal of Inflammation. J Inflamm (Lond). Sep 27 2004;1(1):1. doi:10.1186/1476-9255-1-1

2.   Kulie T, Groff A, Redmer J, Hounshell J, Schrager S. Vitamin D: an evidence-based review. J Am Board Fam Med. Nov-Dec 2009;22(6):698-706. doi:10.3122/jabfm.2009.06.090037

3.   Japelt RB, Jakobsen J. Vitamin D in plants: a review of occurrence, analysis, and biosynthesis. Front Plant Sci. 2013;4:136. doi:10.3389/fpls.2013.00136

4.   Laird E, McNulty H, Ward M, et al. Vitamin D deficiency is associated with inflammation in older Irish adults. J Clin Endocrinol Metab. May 2014;99(5):1807-15. doi:10.1210/jc.2013-3507

5.   Coussens AK, Martineau AR, Wilkinson RJ. Anti-Inflammatory and Antimicrobial Actions of Vitamin D in Combating TB/HIV. Scientifica (Cairo). 2014;2014:903680. doi:10.1155/2014/903680

6.   Holick MF. Sunlight and vitamin D for bone health and prevention of autoimmune diseases, cancers, and cardiovascular disease. Am J Clin Nutr. Dec 2004;80(6 Suppl):1678S-88S. doi:10.1093/ajcn/80.6.1678S

7.   Holick MF. Vitamin D deficiency. N Engl J Med. Jul 19 2007;357(3):266-81. doi:10.1056/NEJMra070553

8.   Commins SP, Borish L, Steinke JW. Immunologic messenger molecules: cytokines, interferons, and chemokines. Journal of Allergy and Clinical immunology. 2010;125(2):S53-S72.

9.   Zhang Y, Leung DY, Richers BN, et al. Vitamin D inhibits monocyte/macrophage proinflammatory cytokine production by targeting MAPK phosphatase-1. J Immunol. Mar 1 2012;188(5):2127-35. doi:10.4049/jimmunol.1102412

10.   Nielsen FH, Johnson LK, Zeng H. Magnesium supplementation improves indicators of low magnesium status and inflammatory stress in adults older than 51 years with poor quality sleep. Magnes Res. Dec 2010;23(4):158-68. doi:10.1684/mrh.2010.0220

11.   Rubin LP, Ross AC, Stephensen CB, Bohn T, Tanumihardjo SA. Metabolic Effects of Inflammation on Vitamin A and Carotenoids in Humans and Animal Models. Adv Nutr. Mar 2017;8(2):197-212. doi:10.3945/an.116.014167

12.   Trumbo P, Yates AA, Schlicker S, Poos M. Dietary reference intakes: vitamin A, vitamin K, arsenic, boron, chromium, copper, iodine, iron, manganese, molybdenum, nickel, silicon, vanadium, and zinc. J Am Diet Assoc. Mar 2001;101(3):294-301. doi:10.1016/S0002-8223(01)00078-5

13.   Ebina K, Shi K, Hirao M, et al. Vitamin K2 administration is associated with decreased disease activity in patients with rheumatoid arthritis. Mod Rheumatol. Sep 2013;23(5):1001-7. doi:10.1007/s10165-012-0789-4

14.   Oliviero F, Spinella P, Fiocco U, Ramonda R, Sfriso P, Punzi L. How the Mediterranean diet and some of its components modulate inflammatory pathways in arthritis. Swiss Med Wkly. 2015;145:w14190. doi:10.4414/smw.2015.14190

15.   Gu Y, Zhao A, Huang F, et al. Very low carbohydrate diet significantly alters the serum metabolic profiles in obese subjects. J Proteome Res. Dec 6 2013;12(12):5801-11. doi:10.1021/pr4008199

16.   Szeto YT, Kwok TC, Benzie IF. Effects of a long-term vegetarian diet on biomarkers of antioxidant status and cardiovascular disease risk. Nutrition. Oct 2004;20(10):863-6. doi:10.1016/j.nut.2004.06.006

17.   Ziegler D, Hanefeld M, Ruhnau KJ, et al. Treatment of symptomatic diabetic polyneuropathy with the antioxidant alpha-lipoic acid: a 7-month

multicenter randomized controlled trial (ALADIN III Study). ALADIN III Study Group. Alpha-Lipoic Acid in Diabetic Neuropathy. Diabetes Care. Aug 1999;22(8):1296-301. doi:10.2337/diacare.22.8.1296

18. Panahi Y, Alishiri GH, Parvin S, Sahebkar A. Mitigation of Systemic Oxidative Stress by Curcuminoids in Osteoarthritis: Results of a Randomized Controlled Trial. J Diet Suppl. 2016;13(2):209-20. doi:10.3109/19390211.2015.1008611

19. Karimi N, Dabidi Roshan V, Fathi Bayatiyani Z. Individually and Combined Water-Based Exercise With Ginger Supplement, on Systemic Inflammation and Metabolic Syndrome Indices, Among the Obese Women With Breast Neoplasms. Iran J Cancer Prev. Dec 2015;8(6):e3856. doi:10.17795/ijcp-3856

20. Shih CM, Cheng SN, Wong CS, Kuo YL, Chou TC. Antiinflammatory and antihyperalgesic activity of C-phycocyanin. Anesth Analg. Apr 2009;108(4):1303-10. doi:10.1213/ane.0b013e318193e919

THANK YOU
FOR FINISHING THE BOOK!

We would like to thank you very much for supporting us and reading through to the end. We know you could have picked any number of books to read, but you picked this book and for that, we are extremely grateful.

We hope you enjoyed your reading experience. If so, it would be really nice if you could share this book with your friends and family by posting on Facebook and Twitter.

Happy Health Publishing stands for the highest reading quality and we will always endeavor to provide you with high-quality books.

Would you mind leaving us a review on Amazon before you go? Because it will mean a lot to us and support us in creating high-quality guidelines for you in the future.

Please help us reach more readers by taking 30 seconds to write just a few words on Amazon now.

REVIEW ME

Warmly yours,
The Happy Health Publishing Team

IF YOU'VE ENJOYED
THE ANTI-INFLAMMATORY VITAMIN MADE EASY,
YOU'LL ALSO ENJOY IN THIS SERIES:

EPSTEIN-BARR VIRUS FOR BEGINNERS:
Find out how to Fight The Epstein-Barr Virus And Chronic Fatigue Syndrome With The Right Treatment Of EBV.

https://amzn.to/3uuuPQ3*

FUN AND WEIRD MEDICAL FACTS:
10 Amazing Facts About the Human Body You Have Never Thought of.

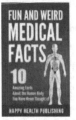 

https://amzn.to/3utQ44u*

Made in United States
Troutdale, OR
03/15/2024

18488276R00030

COMPLETE GUIDE
ON HOW TO PLAY THE
Harmonica

Harmonica Harmony: Unleashing the Soulful
Sounds of the Blues in Your Hands(Teach Yourself
to Play)

ISAK QUENTIN